# FLOWERS OF RAIN

## POEMS TO TOUCH YOUR SOUL

### PURBESH MAHAPATRA

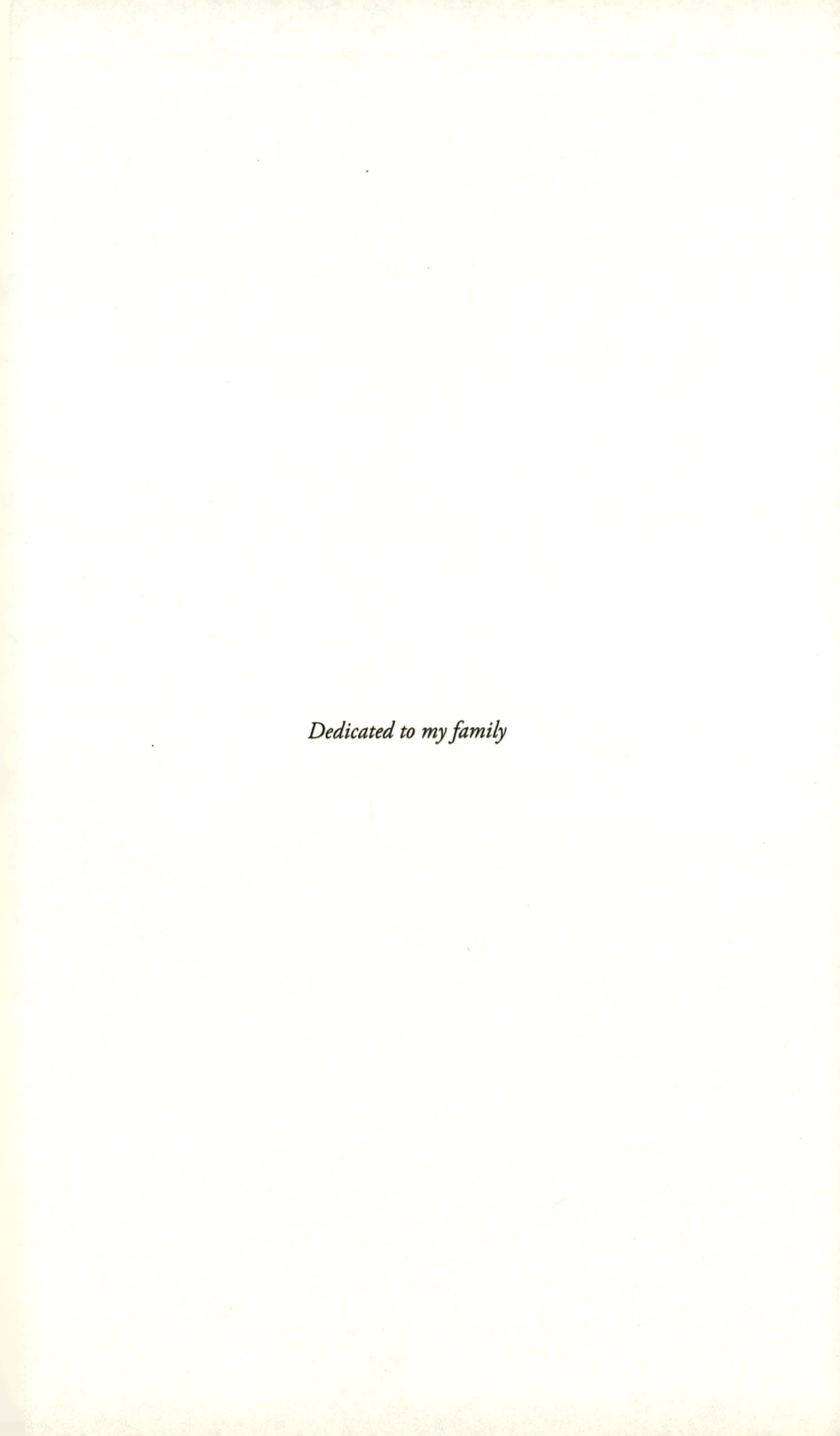

*Dedicated to my family*

# Contents

# Contents

# Contents

# Contents

# Foreword

Love and gratitude to the reader

# Preface

*A journey is starting...*

# Acknowledgements

My sincere thanks to Nature.

# Prologue

What is poetry but mind blood.

# 1. A moonless night

A humming blackness exists in layers
By an icy riverside in the Himalayas
Far on rum and applesin
To the stars in my view I smile
I greet and ask how do you do
They all laugh as lions
In deafening quantum silence
They tell me they are great watchers
And are mystical life light throwers
I hear the river splash and slush
I feel the waves rise and rush
The smell of the old mountains
Invites lovingly the stray rains

# 2. A rolling stone knows what moss it gathers

God has shown me my destination
Have to keep moving to reach in time
I do not build houses in town or heart
Because I know I cannot stay long
Anxiety sets in when I take a little rest
The mysterious unknown chews the brain
And a new life begins like a bud blooming
With the dew in the morning sun rays
New rivers are crossed to take new roads
Reaching out to new people and homes
Saying goodbye is all my heart fears
Because a rolling stone hates tears

# 3. A shy morning

You can but can I leave you alone
A dew fell from the lifeless leaf alone
Dark clouds swallowed every morning
My hope to see the sun this morning
You could not come through the storm
My misfortunes came with the storm
The silent shore told the wolf at night
Memories of that morning hunt all night

# 4. A wandering planet with no sun

I am cold but not at heart
There is been no one from the start
To show me the light
And teach me the right path to life
Only the envy warms my surface sometimes
Whenever I pass close by solar systems
Otherwise it is been a lonely long story
Pity I cannot kill myself

# 5. Alexander

Restless waters moved on
As Alexander eyed the horizon
Victory was on his tongue
And he smelt many bloods
He thought hungrily of
The most glorious honor
And of land of the golden sands
As it lay fantastically behind enemy lines
When the time came
And the distance shortened
For Alexander to fix his eyes
On the mighty armies of India
He felt as a bitch in the jungle among lions
When the winter was starting
To eat the earth in maya
Dreams shattered as sweet Greek love
Turned into the image of Hephaestion
Alexander sent his cavalry to heroism
Little knowing they would go so far
And when his mighty ego lay in a pool
Of blood of mankind and peace
The poor king ran with a squeak
Without his soul he died quick

# 6. Anonymous hitman

No one liked him much from his childhood
He kept all his secrets to himself
As there was no one to talk to
The kindred spirited people
He did not meet any
His loved ones eaten in war
His beloved country lost to dark forces
His only way out was to become a killer

# 7. An aimless life

Staring across the rushing river
I looked beyond the shore farther
To see the setting sun in the horizon
Calling me for a night on the other side
Dreaming of what riches and fame lay there
I forgot all and everything on this side
And dived into the torrid black waters
Though the waves were mountainous
And the current a relentless sea of ghosts
They could to a stone heart do no harm
I reached the far shore drenched in sweat
And ran out like a pilgrim nearing his shrine
The wonders of Thee lay graciously there
I learnt many things and cherished the journey
Crossing hills and troughs I wandered to a shore
Of a river like the old blacker still and hissing more

# 8. An evening in Zanskar

The vague images of dreams
Rise up again in my mind
After a long sunny day
With the frosty evening wind
In this unending stretch
Of rock snow and the skies
Memories sketch a muddy river
Through the dark grim valleys
The black of the night and
The heavy waves of the river
Spell my soul to leave me
And wander to the river shore
My soul turns back and
Looks at me very sadly
I feel the chill of sadness
And beg him to return promptly

# 9. An unquiet mind

It seems as if yesterday
All was fine
I was laughing
And having a good time
There were scores of friends to meet everyday
And heavenly food to eat all day
Nice clothes to wear
A father and mother to care
Secret places to explore
And dare the fear
To go beyond the rules
And give guilt a miss
This beautiful world it seems
As if it was only yesterday

# 10. Artificial diamond

With some money I had saved for my palace
I bought a diamond for my charming princess
From deep under the sands of a river tributary
Had obtained a crocodile hunter a rare solitary
He sold it to an exorcist for two healthy goats
Which became mine with few bundles of notes
In the dusk and dawn the stone from the sky
Changed colors to royal blue to a greenish shy
And with morning sun the cerulean hue returned
Starting from the core and spreading all around
The hazy sky stone had taken my heart away
I felt the extraordinary joy in her heart of clay
How this can be earthly exceeded my learning
I felt like I possessed a power beyond a king
Things so got out of my hands it so conspired
As often happens with matters of mind and heart
In the gift I had kept for her to seal the love bond
I replaced the sky stone with an artificial diamond

# 11. Ashoka scheme

In the midst of a creepy night
Jackals howl a plan of deceit
The poverty of humanity
At their ominous doorsteps
Allures them to spin fancy tales
In India they would explicitly
Pull out the seating lion from air
Old magic reborn a master plan
The white beasts shoveled hard
From the Indus to Kalinga
And all the way to Sri Lanka
To bury truth with lies on stone
From where and when was he born
The quantum knowledge his mother had not known
The teachers of children in this great country
Had tongues of black Karma
The leaders saved the flames of lies
Their coffers filled in gold and sapphires
Long and hard the albino has schemed
To make us unaware that we have been tricked
But we the children of Bharat Mata
Will bury the legacy of fake Ashoka
Way deeper than his wretched edicts
Once again truth will conquer time predicts

# 12. As hungry as a shark

I am a great shark
Lonely but not dangerous
Just kidding as in smiling
I promise no laughing
I am very weak in emotions
Hardly one discerns me in all oceans
The magnificence of my senses
The audacity in my defenses
My shark brain and untiring eyes
Deeply impress all my enemies
All great ones have only me to idolize
Immortalizing my legacy in unending seas
I am the revolution of creation
The weapon of evolution
I always seem to be praying
As seems God is always listening
In deepest and coldest water
I lie low the unseen terror
I float like a cherished dream
I am by Nature most extreme
Better known across the seven seas
In all directions trenches and keys
The cold-hearted legend of killing
The most fearsome end to beginning
Since long I have realized

No life ever sees me coming
Once I had a friend
Now he is dead
Pierced in all sides
Blood redding the tides
Humans killed my crony
My ally I know not why
This event caught fancy of my heart
When it broke apart part by part
Maybe killed to eat but you see
Now I have more for me
I am neither a virtuoso
Or either a swindler by nature
I have been starving yesterday
At present and in future
I do not kill by deceit
I execute by my merit
I move like a whip of lightning
To unleash death upon living
The setting sun raises the heat
A tuna or mackerel will be a treat
A great place is this sea in dark
Greater still is the hunger of a shark

# 13. Baikal and Lena

My love for you overflows the shadows of imagination
In a dark bar in Siberia at dawn
Mixing whisky and vodka since the night before
Friends from far lands have come
To see the tidings of hearts and fates
They have come not hiding
Nor they came for the certain danger
The false chaos of the noises
The shy bulbs in the corners
Aimless shadows bending and vanishing
Wherever eyes went to see nothing
Rounded tables in that place
Tell in mysterious ways to keep drinking
I looked at the watch and felt for my rifle
Let today it not be put to use
I am just waiting for someone to come
My last ride will last until my home
The Lord will not forgive
The sins of me and my friends
The paths of life like roots of trees
One such end of the road
Starts from this very black building
I hear my friends rejoice in bliss
As the north wind blasts the windows beside me
The gales of heartbeats run wild and free

A sad heart when feels strong
Tears of joy roll along
All pains vanish and fancy ambitions
As our eyes meet to ask for directions
The ale maker will keep a heavy fee
I pay in silvers and tip in gold
Till my pockets are empty

# 14. Beers of Europe

Right there when you get lonely
You remember a friend suddenly
Who comes from another land
And tells mysterious stories and legends
It is time to call upon
And hold the door open
To the little beer cavern
For your lonely dear friend
Let the dark beers run in the breath
Beers dark as the night of death
Listen to the music
Tap your feet and swing your head
Throw your hands away
And dance to the groovy music
Let the love grip you tight
Let the mind howl to night
Free birds have gone to nests
Two more big jugs my friend requests
Like the black poisonous love of a witch
The dark amber brew refuses to relent
Deep into the freezing night
Dancing under the flying snow
We wander through the slippery streets
Singing the famous beer song beats

# 15. Before dying the soldier didn't cry

He remembered the faces of his mother
and little sister and thought that
he will miss her marriage
and playing with her kids
in the hills chasing rabbits
He remembered his father
and bowed in respect and gratitude
and forgave him and asked pleadingly
for his forgiveness so that he can die in peace
And then he closed his eyes
and saw the beautiful smiling face of his mother
kissing him and just when he felt
he was only a few moments away
he saw the face of the girl of his dreams
her smooth face innocent smile shallow dark eyes
and her lips like a remembered dream
and felt happy that he had kept his feelings
and now all that he could see
was a brightly burning cold light
that was everywhere around him
and he could feel the muscles in his forehead relax and breathing stop

# 16. Birds on trees

A nest calls the little bird since dawn
Perhaps it is noon by now
Come back screech the tiny ones
In hunger to see their mother
Beyond hills and river valleys
Inside the dark jungles of mystery
The little bird searches for prey
Unaware of the hawk that might be lurking
Uncaring of the viper that could be hunting
Unknown of the time of the day
One by one minutes fall as time passes away
In empty stomach she collects the scarce prey
Friends of the little bird console the tiny ones
One says the little bird is already on the way
If only the tiny ones had known their language
They would have been silent a long time by
Friends of the little bird share a few worms
And the tiny ones call it a day just for a moment
To yearn for their mother straight away
When the wind changes from west to north
The little bird glides through the trees and branches
Into the waiting nest and drops a mouthful of worms
On the plates of wary and hungry residents

# 17. Bonfire in jungle

Troubled around leaping smoke
And thinking of friends and folk
The river smiles with silver foam
Under the beaming moon fish roam
My heart beats like a smoking guitar
In sync with the leaps of molten fire
I pour my eye into the golden flames
Like on a mirror I see my sad face
The burnt flowers spent dreams evoke
Higher and higher I move from desire
I breathe in the fire and let out the smoke
My cold heart warms up to thank the bonfire

# 18. Captain Soul speaking

It gives me great joy that we finally meet
I know you too feel the same
I hope love is swell and all well
We are sad but do not cry
The rough seas not many have seen
Through dark valleys fewer have been
Keep courage in your heart
Honor always in your eyes
And seek for strength in your mind
From the all merciful One
Please do not ask my stories
Yours is my story now
We have long journeys to make
And many roads to take
For the sake of you I say
Let us live it the right way

# 19. Colors of nature

The disciple of nature bowed his shaven head
Inflated his chest for a deep breath
And gazed deep into the horizon from edge of the mountain
To see beyond the skin that he wore

# 20. Devi Rukmini

We pray to goddess Rukmini
The divine queen of Lord Krishna
When love wrote in blood
In a language of eternity
From the hand of goddess
Our all-powerful Lord
Became overwhelmed
In timeless contentment
The angel on Earth
The most beautiful queen
The soul of Mother
In kindness and virtue
With no equal in Bharata
Had expressed Her love
In a resolute decision
To unite with Lord forever
With enemies galore
Faith answered once more
When the last breath
Of hope had drowned
Our fearless Lord
Made His promise true
The celestial princess
Where glory adorned Her feet
Took the hand of the Lord

To make Him Her forever
The greatest of kings
The fiercest of warriors
In defeat they burned
Empty handed they returned
When union of two souls happen
The love of our Lord has spoken
For the only one that She is always
The singular love of Lord Krishna

# 21. Difference between a song and a poem

Would you seek melody in a song
And may not find rhyme in a poem
That you so much love singing
Would you care to write a poem
The song touched your soul I know
Did the poem say something your heart wanted to tell
To you and me and for the world the song is
A poem from the broken heart of the poet

# 22. Electric pain



Sweet love caught me
And left me far far away
To be somebody
I hardly recognized yesterday

# 23. Few lines from a prayer

When will man stop
Abusing mother nature
When will man stop
Exploiting each other
When will man start
Winning by truth
When will man start
Gaining with faith
O Maker of natural laws
I ask You this because
You are the Lord
You are the God
Of bliss and agony

# 24. Flowers of rain

I had some money then
When love was cheap and roads narrow
I lost myself one such way
As of losing I have this only to say
Of all things lost I remembered
Foremost were the flowers of rain
The clouds hung low at each turn
Below the mountainous sky
Asked the stranger as she looked away
Have you seen my butterflies fly by
The rain fell before she smiled and said
My swallowtails cherish the rain beloved
Where it started and whence it will end
On which peak didn't it rain
Deep from the river valley the mist soared
Unending upon thirsty earth the rain poured
Drawn into the battle of earth her and rain
How it felt in senses as love dawned again
The smiles on her face went on and on
She began as I had to feel no more alone
The lilac golden and blue butterflies
From the hazy sky rained with the rain
Upon the flowers rain had set free
They have come back to meet her said she
In the rain in sad vein when in deep pain

What I remember most are the flowers of rain

# 25. From my broken heart

A little thing that blossoms in our hearts
Pure new and full of bliss
Like a flower till it withers away
The same flower never blooms again
And no one remembers it
But the empty stalk that quietly decays

# 26. Gamechanger

All in all we are getting aloner brother
Old age is but one fearful adventure
The sly jackals have hijacked the scepter
And over rule the world with a whip severe
Brother is fighting a war with his brother
Mr Fox become king after they kill each other
The wives and daughters will know torture
And sons trapped and used for plunder
They cut trees and make money from paper
And make the world go round at their order
Their puppets rule over countries and more
No one helps when truth calls murder murder
Have eyes do we have the power to see brother
Through many fake religion and fake messenger
The voice of universal music is lost in disorder
And the connection to God it feels is past forever
The abusers of humanity live in castles of wonder
No economist knows why poor are becoming poorer
Humanity bleeds in unseen numbers to win a war
And who gains over the dead bodies tell me dear
Is it the global banker or the war hawking bloodsucker
Or the serum seller or the international weapon maker
His dominance over the planet is complete as ever
No one hears the poor man howling robber robber
It is time to remove your frocks of fear brother

Do not leisure yourself on your trust in God to deliver
When soldiers die they do not know the truth bitter
That they did not die for their beloved nation mother
Burn the manifestos both red and green for they error
Written by slaves of Mr Fox they hide the true picture
It is time to remove the blindfold from justice figure
And noose the traitors so in hell they may prosper
Do not let the sacrifices of ancestors go in failure
The vultures shriek in anticipation for the end is near
Conquer the battlefields and kill the devil with fear
No one believes a foxy player crying gamechanger

# 27. Gratitude for the Game

From what thought came the love to play

Why was it necessary for God

to transform Himself into the universe

Why God is so powerful

What is the illusion of wormholes and dimensions

What is beyond the walls of this universe

Sometimes God gets emotional too

And flashes it in full measure

What makes God think He can do all this

Even if there is no one to stop Him

Will it have been better

if God existed only in Himself

Will it have been better

if there were no stars no night no Sun and Moon

No Earth no trees no seas no birds no flowers

No beasts and mountains no rivers and cultures

Without time and love and music and mysteries

And mothers and brothers and without you and me

Will it have been better

if God existed only in Himself

# 28. Happy New Day

Live everyday
And love
And celebrate life everyday
For it comes just once everyday
Every morning on an everyday
Wish yourself
Happy New Day

# 29. Har Har Gange

Maa Ganga we offer you our salutations
Ganga dropped on earth
In the north of Garhwal
As a great bomb of snow
On the matted locks of Shiv Shankar
Holy water burst from four places
From the Char Dham of Uttarakhand
Bhagirathi by Gangotri
Mandakini from Kedarnath
Alaknanda through Badrinath
Yamuna at Yamunotri
All hungry to merge
At the right place
At the right moment
To bridge Ganga the holiest
From the feet of Vishnu
In the land of Badri
Covered in snow cold as loneliness
Where grass grew with a certain fineness
Passing by Panch Prayag
Paces raging and restless
Alaknanda gives while faceless
From the third eye of Shambhu
Springs the purest water
Deep in love the divine waters

Yearning and burning she wanders
Through many a merciless turn
Rolling on white foam
Mandakini bravely moves on
From the lap of snowy peaks
Her sisters she greatly seeks
Like a blue unstopping snake
Entwined upon an earthly angel
Flowing among the empyrean mountains
Cutting across chains and healing sins
Bhagirathi slithers through the stony inclines
Mandakini dissolves within Alaknanda
As Rudra and Chamunda
Under the rock of Narada
In the holy fork of Rudraprayag
The spirit of Alaknanda
Slips into the aura of Bhagirathi
To give birth to Ganges almighty
At the godly spot of Devprayag
Unending in blessings
Unremitting in healings
Unasked she provides
Lovingly she enlightens
What have we ungrateful achieved
Little of good and lot of bad
Dams that kill all Her fish
And to think of funny ideas
As to interlink our mother river
And cheat the destiny of living water

# 30. Healing the wound of betrayal

Life is beautiful and the time is here
Forgive yourself and the betrayer
At their doors leave a letter of adieu
And remember them who stood by you
Love who loved in unconditional ways
Thank the ever generous One always
A new road waits for you longingly
New friends seek you unknowingly
Let faith come into your lionheart
Say the old prayers before you start
Look at the rising Sun in His eyes
It is Your turn now to touch the skies

# 31. Highland wanderers



The hills call after sad longings
And wild birds howl during noises
The cold rivers rush on the horizons of daydreams
And the flowers blush upon view
We will meet someday on ways through the highlands
Namaste to all fellow pathfinders
In the journey we shall bond like brothers
And make a cult of nature lovers

# 32. Home has no adjective before it

In my life I have seen two kinds of many people

Those who have home and all other types of people

What pain and joy it brings to the heart

To think of a past home or

Seeing homes on the path of time

Lovely and radiant and filled in noises

Pity I do not have a home

A place to call my own

I stay in rooms and move often

Silence stays with me in my home

And when I venture outside

It always clings to me that I

Have a sad face that I

Do not have a home of my own

When noises and light fill up homes around me

I get soaked in guilt and loneliness

That cringes my heart

And asks humiliating questions at my soul

# 33. i for introspection

Have I hurt an unselfish heart
Have I forgotten a helping hand
Have I repented a wrong choice
Have I understood a stifled voice
Who is the soul in my soul
Who is the winner when I reach my goal
Who makes me fearless of death
Who when penniless puts the bread
What is beyond my image
What is this mirage
What do not I see
What always sees me
Why do I feel love in my broken heart
When will time restart
Why do I question
Where is the answer

# 34. I remember You

I remember you
You are the only one who said
I love you too

# 35. I think I lost the game and more

I feel the devil is troubling me
Numbing my brain and hunger
Can you check can you see me
I think I lost the game and more

# 36. I was a mad man

Hungry lonely and without peace years went by
Trying to find the destiny that I had lost midway
Many learned humans I made know on the way
Though many spake of the One none could justify
Until I met an old sailor who told marvelous stories
Of science and Gods and of astonishing mysteries
Only the truth can set you free
Said my new teacher to me
And holding my trembling hands
He showed how in heart cometh Thee
By the yellow light of glory
Spreading from his forehead
I followed his footsteps until
I could finally see the light
My gratitude to my teacher to walk
All through the darkness for me

# 37. Indian Tiger



If beauty was a beast
She would be a tiger

# 38. Julay

When in the mountains of India
If you hear julay tell julay
If you do not hear then certainly tell julay
One world word means
Welcome
How are you
I am glad to see you
I am well
Bless you
Bless us
Thank you
All is well
Goodbye
Have a safe journey
See you soon
So long take care
We are grateful to meet
The word heals the mind and lifts the spirit
JULAY

# 39. League of sons of thieves

The exclusive club lies like a nest
In the deep tress by the lake to west
If love would have been here she would say
Interesting place how did I miss by the way
Day and night it belongs to the ghosts
Who wear masks and do not rest
Their strange cars make a lot of sound
Their peculiar pursuit of gold is unbound
They work hard at night to dare by the day
So they have no need to hide their ranks
You can almost find them by the way
In the corner offices of the tallest banks

# 40. Let the storm come



Let the storm come
It is about time
Let the storm know
It is not my first time
Let the storm come
To blow me away
To the storm I say
Go home baby else stay

# 41. Listen to me my love

Listen to me my love
You are the most desirable girl in this town
I and all men of young age rise sharp at dawn
To see you go to the temple to offer your prayers
And wait till you come back with sleepy eyes
When you walk my heart beats with each step
When you take a turn at the corner of the road
My heart slowly stops as the dress embraces
The heavenly shape of your body
I follow you every morning to your home
The gate at my college is full of blooming faces
Who study here and from colleges far away
Everyone is waiting when from the far right road
Through the golden rays shredded by the flame trees
You will come walking with your friends
Bets are placed in stampedes of your dress color
But amidst all these foolish lovers I am the only one
Who loves you truly
This is a small town my love
Never since the universe began
Has a beautiful girl like you set foot on this land
You are the daughter and the mother of this town
And if you become my wife how lucky I will be
Hundreds roar and burst my dream into air
You enter the ghostly arch all the while

Looking at your feet
As you feel too much shame to raise your eyes
And show your godly face to these salivating pigs
When all see you looking at your feet
Everyone looks at your feet too
As you vanish into the grey building
All close their eyes and there is a saddest silence
Of lovers from other colleges mourning the most
As they now have to leave for their own college
But no one knows the truth that I know
You will be moving to a big city any day now
Which is best for your future
I have been trying to speak to you
Since a long time
Long time I have been holding my words
In this vast world I seem to be growing smaller
You are like the rose bud in that deep forest
That blooms for ever till it is touched
So please my love do not let anyone
Be too close to you so that they may
Bleed by the thorns and put the blame on you
And you like a cake of butter in fire
With a heart like newborn calf
Will not be able to see the cunning in the eyes
Of this wolf in city manners
You will not remember me as the city
Will give you a new life
Will your beauty grow and you will be
More beautiful in the city

How many more will fall in love with you
Will there be someone who could love you
As much as I do
If I meet someone such one day
I will make him my best friend in the day
And hear your beauty as words from him
In the night I will leave him to his miseries
But listen to this my love
Tomorrow when you leave
All laughs of innocent love will be soundless
In this small town

# 42. Little son

Our little son is very cute and bubbly
Soft and docile like the heart of a baby
Adored by all he forgets to love back often
Though people do not mind at all
He keeps apologizing again and again
Heart full of hope and love
He inspires the crestfallen
When none dare to aid the weak
Little son helps the wronged with no fear
To the poor he is their secret wealth
And to friends and family their very breath
Great God be always kind on little son
May your place be forever safe in heaven

# 43. Love at first sight

I hope I could explain you
It would have been a song
For lovers around the world
Who cared a damn for gold
I feel I should love you
It may have been the wind
Coming from the icy lands
For it deep froze my bones
I think I ought to tell you
It must have been the truth
That love for you will not end
If you say yes to my request
I know I can love you
It must have been the heart
That stopped and boomed
Exactly when love started

# 44. Maharathi Arjuna

When the golden Bharata
Was burdened in adharma
Lord Vishnu sent an arrow
From His golden bow Krishna
And named the arrow Arjuna
Son of the mighty Indra
Weilder of the Gandiva
The most admirable Pandava
The center of Mahabharata
The last great warrior of Dharma
The alter ego of Hrishikesha
The eternal friend of Narayana
The preacher of Satya karma
The tallest hero of Kurukshetra
The slayer of Suryaputra Karna
The all powerful Phalguna
The fearless vanquisher the favourite pupil
Of the unconquerable Bhisma
The unrivaled archer the finest disciple
Of the infallible Drona
The knower of all music
The Lord of sleep
The fury of Shiva
The wisdom of Brahma
The mortal incarnation of Nara

In the all encompassing Triloka
There was never a Dhanurdhara
As the blessed valorous Dhananjaya
The most handsome man
Invulnerable as the Banyan
The final frontier of warfare
Never fought a battle unfair
The darling of immortal Gods
The conqueror of darkness
The winner of immeasurable wealth
The receptor of divine knowledge
The creator of fear
The divine enchanter
The ultimate lover
The paragon father
The Guru of Satyaki
Ardent son of Kunti
The subduer of enemy
The diffuser of sorcery
The master of Tantra
The teacher of Veda
The chosen knower of Vishwarupa
Partha the beloved of Vasudeva
Apple of the eye of Madhusudana

# 45. Manifesto of children of India

No apathy

No poverty

No corruption

No exploitation

No violence

No trafficking

No drugs

Yes God

Yes Dharma

Yes Indian

Yes Peace

Yes Culture

Yes Education

Yes Best in the world

# 46. Miracles do happen all the time

On a lovely still spring morning

Some hours and fewer birds had flown by

White sheets of rock and snow

Mixed errorlessly with the pacific sky

As songs and music of old days gone by

The pines firs and the occasional oak

Covered in the halcyon snows of smoke

In midst spread a small lake

As blue as poison as a whist snake

It calmed my mind and assured no heartache

In darkness I could see

The motion of earth around the sun

In space She was not free

To choose it's own direction

But mimic an equation

The sun whizzed and rose in angles

Against the starry black night

The round planets whirled and wobbled

No one hurried and nothing was troubled

The planets rolled like bullets

And the comets cried like witches

The symphony of creation

The furious forces of rotation

The chaos manifested in desperate emptiness

Throughout eternal time and infinite space
The amazing universe worked relentless
Unrested and egoless
In constant change but nevertheless
The lake was as calm
As a forgotten tombstone
Silent as deeds undone
I opened my eyes and realized
Miracles do happen all the time

# 47. Money is never enough

In a dream I saw that all the seas and oceans
were filled with money yet people were sad
They missed the old sea terribly and the sea gales
The fish eating birds shrieked frenziedly
against the flint colored sky
People from everywhere had lined up the shores
To take a look at this miraculous crisis
That could end all human wants
The air was still and emotions stirred in hearts
The calmness hung like a heavy dry canvas in hot sun
No one spoke and no one touched a paper of money
We all looked at it as if it was indispensable
The sea of money unending like the sky itself
Lay there stretched to eternities

# 48. Much wandering I had to do

I do not stay to water the seeds sown
In wild they lived a life of their own
Wondering where the wanderer went
In what ways his days were spent
It burns a pain so deep away in emptiness
That friends like you fill in happiness
I so desire to be a king of all little places
That are in your hearts of holiness
Life slept a night of death to see the sun rise again
Bliss filled into the painful heart of the reborn
And my soul told to the wanderer
Now you are no more a stranger

# 49. My first pair of jeans

The cloudy day finally arrived
With love to my first pair of jeans
Of ashen colors it burned
When white lost into grey sins
The black from an oak fire pit
Was the color of my bike
It contrasted with uber swag hit
Pasted against the jeans I liked
The rains blasted from the dark skies
Speeds in my mind slipped time
Quite carelessly floating on the grey roads
Biking ghostly towards a future crime
The bliss in my heart with raindrops
With the lost wind and my new jeans
Made my soul soak my happiness in closed eyes
With a screech and thud
On the very first day
I ruined my first pair of jeans

# 50. My heart paints

My heart paints
Symbols of love
Colors of dreams
In blood
My heart paints
Our fears
Our hopes
For freedom
My heart paints
The pain within
The beauty outside
To live

# 51. My life my shadow

The legs of the spider
Move on the shadows of the web
The wind feels like time
Coming and going without wasting time
The butterflies try to say something
And why the moths are so feisty
The spider is the web
The web spins unseen
The web waits
Like a frozen stream
Strung between trees
Sometimes looking up to the sky
And watching the animals pass by
The spider wonders
Is someone watching me
A predator like the silent dawn
Someone darker than my web
Perhaps a shadow of my life

# 52. My white umbrella

Rain clouds surged towards the eye
Like monstrous alligators in ashen skins
Sucked into a black whirlpool of thunder
With lightnings streaking the changing sky
Over the green and dark wilderness
Of a thousand genus of life
The raven haired maelstrom
Pulled the sky from all directions
The narrow dark skinned roads
Slithered amongst the lazy hills
I looked up at the center of the storm
As it hovered angrily over my destination
What high magic made the sky lose her color
For the day on that road I was the last traveler
My unplanned journey to this unseen place
Coerces on the dipping sun to pick up my pace
Dark tree branches marquee the sunlight away
It feels ghoulish in a very strange way
I voyage alone and afraid through the isolation
Deep into the belly of natural civilization
Blasts of raindrops charge through sparse leaves
Making me sea wet and my view blurry
Everywhere the dense mists fill up the vacuity
I struggle hard on the turn due to the acclivity
In a little distance I was surprised to see

What looked like another human being to me
A sad looking face struggled to have a glance
As we looked on blankly at this happenstance
As I realized her misfortune in the storm
I hurriedly reached for my forgotten umbrella
Barely poor to save her from the rainstorm
Yet may be enough to make her journey manageable
I would not wait for her gratitude
As I looked back at the last turn
She was holding a white umbrella
And looking at me very calmly
Her eyes shined like diamonds
In a fleeting instance of eyesight
I filled my thoughts of the pass
And found myself at the destination
The rains receded as mysteriously
And the evening was as sunny as it could be

# 53. Nikola Tesla is smiling

• 64 •

The mysterious genius lies deep in enigma of obscurity
Away from love and humble respect
The people of this world have sweet remembrance
of the deep silent eyes and his mind for physics
His fight may have been with the world banker
And the global warlord and he might have lost
His life is light and his soul a path to the heaven
His integrity to mother Earth can never be forgotten

# 54. No one is going to hell

• 65 •

I know one of a secret
Of the path to gates of heaven
The unseen eyes of Karma
Sees all and everything
This life will have cuts many
But never make one unnecessarily
By this you will lose
Ego and attachment
To gain enlightenment
And attain the last unification
Of Atman with the Paramatman

# 55. Once upon a time in Cambodia

One weary night in the green Cambodia
Chasing came the planes from America
Riding the wings of terror
Arrived the mad custodians
And in the name of another
They bombed the Cambodians
Hu ha America had come to rule
To set up the Sunday school
Bloods gathered thickly at blackpool
Fear got scared and peace thoughtful
Flames lept in that dark night
There is no love tonight
Killing is the white man's birthright
Proclaimed the lady with the light
They lit up the forest night after night
Did the humble Cambodians get any respite
All pity in world for the human soul
Could pass through a bullet hole
They paid friends and foes more
In pure hate to kill one another
Kinsfolk came from the borders
To widow sisters and slay brothers
Human had no love for man
Man had no ruth on woman

The power of money and ill will
Merchants of death kings of dollar bill
The cunning jackals of capitol hill
Would stop by nothing but to kill
Not for days neither months nor years
They took a decade to quash the khmers
Not in hundreds nor thousands
Neither by ships or either by lands
The coward americans never in a war fair
Rained bombs on Kampuchea from the air
They killed millions of loving Cambodians
And cursed the peasants for the circumstance
Silent was Angkor and Phnom Penh
In no ever shame
They put all the blame
Of killings in the name
When no evil was left undone
On one good honest person

# 56. Phulbani - song of flowers

A billion flowers have bloomed
In the heart of my soul
Singing eternal melodies
Of nature's love
The weary traveler has arrived
In the land of perfumed air
Chanting orphic hymns
Of the flowers' song

# 57. Portrait of a bird

The painting I saw
In the library of Jacob
Of a dove and eagle
Caught my brain in a soup
All the time I stared
The dove was looking at me
Trying to tell a story
I saw it clearly
A tale of love and pain
Like no other
Caught in the snare
The eagle shrieked in the jungle
All day long and night came
Along with the moon
Throwing light on the pain
Of the poor eagle
No bird would dare
To be seen by the hunter of birds
But a little dove
Put so much courage
into her heart
That she flew right
To the eagle paws
And pecking furiously at the snare
Cut it to pieces

To free the mighty eagle
The eagle shrieked and cursed
And in hunger and madness
Put the talons on the neck
Of the innocent little dove
At that very moment
The dove looked at me
From the painting trying
To tell a little story

# 58. Psychology of a ghost

The times of a ghost are always sad
Whoever met a happy ghost are now dead
The fleeting moments of illusion
Take form yet not of matter
Like dim light sources
Wearing their favorite dresses
Float in time without faces
In deep thoughts of past times
In sadness they have made home
Something keeps them heaven from
Their happiness belongs somewhere else
Their pain belongs to only them none else

# 59. Rivers of Bharatavarsh

A million blue and green rivers
Have build trenches into the flesh
Of our motherland sculpting veins
To carry the blood of life
The humble colorless water
The mighty and brave Indus
Cuts between the snowy peaks of Karakoram
And the gorgeous cliffs of Zanskar
Giving life to magical valleys
Of pines deodars and turquoise waters
The supernatural and talismanic Saraswati
Lies hidden in view under the sands of time
Reminding of the flourish of Mohenjodaro and Lothal
The mother of rivers we pray at your feet
Seeking blessings of healing and loving
The holy and pious Ganga
Melts in the heat of love from mankind
And springs from glacial mountains
Taking care of countless souls
More than as a real mother could
The primordial and swift paced Narmada
Sprouting from life creating black stones
Streaks through the highlands heart of India
and between marble valleys and cliff gates
Taking souls and giving souls on the journey

The greatest and wise Mahanadi
Slumbers with determination and faith of a sage
Through the spirituous jungles of eastern India
Holding the sun in the gorgeous green vales
And giving food and boundless joy on the way
The banisher of sins and secluded Papanashini
Ripples through the ethereal hills of Brahmagiri
Between lush green jungles full of elephants
The angelic river of south India needs our care
To again flow in glorious freedom and divine bliss

# 60. Roses in the dusk

Little rose plant
I miss you
My first love
Had a rose of you
Little rose plant
You know my name
We had been friends
When I had none
Little rose plant
Every morning through the window
Every evening
I looked at you

# 61. Scars in the mirror do not heal

The broken wind came unseen
Halting the time for a few moments
All eyes have been thirsty since
The fragrance of your youth spread
The lonely night came unhurried
Burning up dreams with hopes
All feelings have been dead since
The fangs of your eyes teethed
The swift fall came one day
Taking all the pain in life away
All wounds have been healed since
The scars of your smile remained

# 62. Sing a song said my soul



Sing a song said my soul
Cry a pail tonight
Hum a tune now
Kill a guilt while you sleep
Love a moon one day
Feel a pain not yours
Know a truth in conscious faith
Keep a belief in your heart
Pray a God who is the one Om
Know bliss said my soul

# 63. Soul control

Some questions burn at your very soul
Asking questions about your soul
And you know nothing about the soul
Pity it is but let the truth be told
So that you may not let your soul
Be trapped in the world of humans
When death comes finally or unexpectedly
It is time that we have been waiting for
For the holiest moment has arrived to meet God
Fire the element of action and motion
Sends the soul to the kingdom of heaven
This is the ancient rule of creation
For the body to burn after death in cremation

# 64. Story of a lone wolf

The lone wolf had a father
And his father told him
To stick to the lighted path
And follow the righteous life
Lone wolf took all the roads
Except the one his father had said
In hunger of innocent curiosity
And big dreams of worldly powers
He tramped his presence all over
And though he won many things
Peace always seemed to elude away
Lone wolf preyed like a devil possessed
And felt harm would not dare come his way
In his youth he changed many packs
Some he did not like and many time took away
Blacker than his shadow in the night
The heart of lone wolf never saw a bad day
Slowly affairs of seasons rolled on
And lone wolf had won himself a den
On a high mountain cliff in the clouds
And when the full moon came up behind the peaks
Lone wolf howled in his cave in joy
Sending echoes of monstrous weeping through the valleys
That dry night lone wolf fasted towards the drying lake
Shimmering like a fixed mirror in the faint moonlight

It seemed to lone wolf as if a resplendent god stood
Among the dark hell of poisonous forests and strange trees
Lone wolf ambled on the shores towards the lake
Moving gracefully and carefully forward to see a shadow
That looked like a wolf lapping water from a narrow islet
Lone wolf had not seen any wolf for a long time
He growled at the old alien stranger only to be startled
As if he had seen the ghost or the savior of his dreams
The ground gave away and the sounds of nature silenced
Lone wolf recognized the wise eyes of his father
Before the familiar fragrance could reach his nose
The joy and the maddening happiness in his heart
Made the eyes of lone wolf moist and his throat dry
His father embraced him as if he was proud of lone wolf
And lone wolf looked at the moon as if he had found faith

# 65. Sunflowers in moonlight

The evening stormed in from the eastern sky
Covering the sunflower fields in a greyish sheet
Cold rainy winds blew slowly with a mossy scent
This lofty moment felt lordly when the moon appeared
Soon the winter sun rose in the other world
And the moonlight scattered diamond dust
The old oaks stood guard against the cliffs
The smiling petals seemed mysteriously white
Through the purple clouds the moon talked
Beyond the black scabrous face of the cliffs
And the resplendent sunflower fields
Shimmered in such unbound joy and glory
My enchanted heart felt as if I was looking
From the brush of God into a magical painting

# 66. Svarte beach club

The rays of the spring sun
Melt my body into unsubstance
And I feel like a soul
Free from all humanly wants
This land of angels and pious hearts
Of wine lovers and single malts
The long memories of the winters
The blue seas and the warm winds
Stirs up this lonely heart
And entices strangely to depart
From the old bricked university hub
And hit the road to Svarte beach club

# 67. Symbiosis

Good said You have always dragged me down in life
I have been hated because of you
You have made me take the wrong choices
My viewpoint was useless to you
I am mourning on the ruins of your life
You put too much of your world in mine
Bad said I know I have not lived up to your expectations
For the sake of curiosity we broke the frontiers together
The roads we have taken they have taught us who we are
I always selfishly wanted your best more than mine
You need me for the roads are not safe my brother
My world exists on this earth too brother

# 68. Talking to myself

In the start I see
Without seeing actually
By the middle I realize
Myself without disguise
At the end I wonder in doom
Who was talking with whom

# 69. The art of crying

In the darkness of time
A mirror shines so bright
In the calm waters of the soul
I stare myself into the foxhole
The counted ones have forgotten
My soaring dreams have fallen
The road has become scarce
The shady trees growing sparse
I have no shoulder to put my head on
From conventional to myself I run
I was very thirsty one time
I asked a beautiful girl some water
She was not on my way
She watched me pray
And smiled and blushed
Under the stars she hushed
She had water for someone
For her rich white swan
I run a lot to die early
And rest little and poorly
I was on knees in bad time
Hid myself behind a snake pit
When no one could see
All wished to forget me
Where on that deserted road

I never slowed my tears never showed
Through ruination hoping salvation
Towards that desolate destination
I have learnt the art of crying
Is to anticipate a dying

# 70. The coconut grove

The ripe coconut dropped seventy feet
First slowly and then crashing down
On the windshield of an old truck left by
The shield was totally shattered
And the tiny glass pieces had some surprised fun
In the small time the little mayhem brought by
Narrow canals crisscrossed the earthy grounds
And these amazing slender trees grew besides
To great heights almost touching the sky
The roads between them seemed to call
By loud psychological signals to the passerby
Who seek mystery to enter carelessly hereby
The unruly and dangerous jungles beyond
Look astonishingly at the arranged rows
Of beautiful balmy healing coconut trees
And move on with life smiling by

# 71. The cold hearted follower

The boat started to life in the green cold night
Disturbing the thick placid waters of Amazon
The smell of fog and dew filled and chilled us
And made our bones and muscles wind light
As soon as we hit the main river
I fanned all flames and picked up speed
The Russian night goggles helped me
To stay course on the winding veins
Lightnings streaked in blue and pink
On the river surface and the sky
Roared in hunger sometimes then
The morning sun in Manaus waited for us in disfaith
We hope we live through our wounds and hunger till then
My brother grinds his teeth as I pour medicine into the hole in his
stomach
My hands shake in anger and steam from my sweat jam my ears
I look into the wound to seek the enemy bullet though my eyes went
deep
Right down to the dark pit I could not find
I remembered my beautiful house in Tabatinga
And ferries to Iquitos through the dark rainforests
How nature changes slowly all day long and repeats daily
The bullet in the stomach of my brother passes through my heart and
between my eyes every moment
I was dead shot until he came between the bullet and me

I tell my brother not to sleep and keep the wound tight
I hear the jaguar growl and the wolves howl
And meet the electric eyes of the crocodiles
I pray to the all-pervading nature for her blessings
And tearfully hope that the lone healer is in town
My faith in Him is immense
With the morning light and rising sun
My hope receives a hallowed reply
I motor through the wide river like a mad man
Many many friends come and go through time
But my brother is for me and I for him forever
God at your mercy is the gold hearted savior

# 72. The dark side of red

The color of a secret is red
When innocent faith is shed
When a secret is unmade
Your lips become so red
The char of a deep wound
Trickles blood when it could
Love is sold cheap by the dead
Your skin tastes like rye bread
The itch to tell a secret is great
So smoothly to fill a heart with hate
The color of a great love is red
Saved in my heart I had
A sea of love of azure
And waves of passive time
By when thinking of her
My feelings grew madder
But she had plans so sinister
To give my love to a stranger
She was a shade darker than red
My gold of love now lies on seabed
The color of a risk taken is red
A young girl most patiently made
Life wrapped her not in roses
They said she was afraid of failures
Her life shone in places

Yes with some aces
But it not yet so glorious
May be she been notorious
When they judge not knowing
What hell it brings in a risk failing

# 73. The eyes of innocence

Whose eyes are a maze with no escape
The celestial gold of water and fire
Below the titian night thrown to wind
Waters spill jackals howl for the two moons
About them both are brilliant and breathless
The sun was setting on your dream
To right the magnificent sun rose all white
Both the suns stared across my eyes
Your kind eyes the divine prize of all skies
Whose eyes are deep enough to hide a secret
The calm glare the deep stare
Hinged chains forgotten rains
When anythings end and journeys begin
The past is always a way I am not now in
As I learn from your eyes to heart
The place and me know not where we at
Whose eyes I see when I close my eyes
Your innocent eyes

# 74. The fire of revenge

One day revenge came home finally
He was well dressed unlike the unimportant days
And his eyes were very different
As if the storm in his pupils had calmed
I offered food and it made him smile
I could see from his thin wrists
That he needed good rest of nights
And foods to make him better
I told him he can stay here now
And I would feed him and give company
I told him how I had missed him
And he sighed and smiled softly
He thanked me profusely for the food
And the little rest and loving words
He said he will have to leave
And take the boxes of pain with him
For long sad lonely years I had waited
I told him to his face and now without
A heart to heart you are already leaving me
Is that all I have cared for in all these gone times
It is best that I go now said Revenge
I found a teacher many years into the road
And he showed me the path to God
It is time for me to leave your heart
I am sure as God said you will be beautiful without me

I embraced him and felt his warm heart and fragrance
He told me to remember him but never call on
I watched from my eyes his receding figure
Long into the rising sun

# 75. The lion brain

Your eyes play with the light
That puts that lustrous fire in it
This fire then burns in your mind always
Hunger and pride return as the day wakes
The familiar Sun sprays His energy waves
Your roar starts in the hopeless hearts of your prey
You are alive one more day
A poor soul will soon fade away
The family hunts under your command
The highs and lows of the silent ground
The changing light and weather around
Changes in the behavior of the afraid prey
You know your predictions will not betray
The protector demands lion share of buffet
Under your thunderous roar who dares disobey
Tomorrow never came to the hardcore fighters
You realize your mind is just one of your muscles
Compassion you have seen in the eyes of mothers
But compassion is alien to the maned kind
You look at compassion and see things behind
The lions you killed and banished have scarred
Your face and coat bear the signs of deathly fights
For socio political factors and lone personal rights
You ripped all competition apart from your jungle
And sent all them deep into the land of dead

Your leadership over your pride is your pride
You proved yourself as was taught by your father
And mother who many ages ago looked at your eyes
With love and you put your claws deep in her skin
Just to have her attention do you remember
No meal of yesterday can stop the hunger of today
You try to feed your family well and protect everyway
Life changes very fast in the life of a lion they say
The crest of your lifetime will soon complete
Some lions of unmatchable strength
Have been following your scent all night

# 76. The mask collector

The mask shop lies deep and lonely
Between the seven peaks of Solitary
A long narrow snakey road trips roughly
And ends at a ravaged bridge abruptly
I leave my Ducati behind and slide
Down the bank of the stream side
Crossing freezing waters I gently knock
On the wooden door with a mask clock
A horse neighs and I look at the chimney
A thin cloudy tail of smoke rises slowly
And melts with the shadowing evening sky
The cold winds batter hard but there is no reply
The night comes swiftly gobbling all light
I knock again hard and yell with all might
A filament bulb lights up and warms my heart
In anxious anticipation to meet the mask collector
The door wakes slowly and a deep mysterious
Aroma of myrrh and lavender fills up the space
When I was unsure to embrace him or just tell grace
There stood before me a man with a mask on his face

# 77. The purpose of life

There is only one purpose of life
and it is very scientific
All the answer is of quantum physics
the humbling science of God
and in this answer lies a truth
that sets the soul free and unattached
one last time back into the world of Maya
to unite with Om Brahman
fluttering in the same breeze
as the Creator Himself

# 78. The reason of sadness

Is happiness what you want
Were you happy when you got what you wanted
And when you lost it
Did you get sad
Were you happy when someone loved you back
And when love was gone
Did it make you sad
If happiness would not be there
Would sadness be not there too
In the one life we have in this reality
Living through seasons of emotivity
May we be calm in spirit and mind
And treat happiness and sadness in one kind

# 79. The rise of hope

My limitless aspirations
Have taken me everywhere
When my heart wanted to go nowhere
I learnt from the many different paths
That hope is there
For the hopeless like me
As one such path had led to Him

# 80. The strange case of water in Libya

Deep under the burning and scorching Saharan deserts
Where sand dunes play like waves of white silk
Under the Sun and Moon in copious glory of natural fallow
The virgin waters of Nubia once rested in peace
Now the wars on water have started so that water
Can be put a price tag and profits entailed to the locker
Mercy be on the righteous for they may not kill
Hail the new king the evil son of the fake devil

# 81. The sweetest fragrance

In a narrow alley
At a tough left corner
Walking briskly
In dimming lights
When suddenly
I slowed down
Not slowly at all
To the sweet fragrance
Of that unforgettable girl
I changed my road
To follow her
By a hook pierced
Into my heart
By chains it pulled
Merciful with pains
Far greater than I ever had
In my raw imagination
Her name I called
I closed my eyes
To find her way
Sometimes I had to stop
Unwilling and at a loss
As I was melting away
When I found her
I felt a thousand bells ring inside me

I spent the night at her step
By morning I put my heart to stake
The gloomy dawn
And slow rainfall
The chemical phenomenon
Known around as love
All pushed me deep down
Through the waterfall
Never hoped in this ghost town
I will find the mate of my soul
Forever enchanted by the spell
Of sweet fragrance of that girl

# 82. The train to Deomali

The heart of the train
Beats the same rhythm as my heart
As mine excites so hers
My body shakes in anticipation
Of the important journey ahead
A mission at hand
To be completed anyway
However my plans are none
Just a blank brain
In a powerful belief
Hoping for the best

# 83. The truth in a lie

The sound of the mind
Revivals it leaves behind
Of pain and plea
To see no mercy
The hollowness of time
Spent through all life
Deeply saddened my hopes
As life threw no ropes
My little story in the ring
Was like a scorpion sting
The shine of the soul
Tells honestly how I roll
When life seemed a lie
Sometimes I wanted to die
I searched for truth in life
As I believed without it cannot be
I found my helplessness
I watched my circumstances
I visited my ambitions
Between me and a liar all we say
These are the three truths in a lie

# 84. The veil of thirteen

After twelve hours and twelve months
Beyond twelve zodiac star constellations
Arrives a man at number thirteen
The holy seventh number assigns
In the series of divine geometry
To the outstretched arm of thirteen
As far as what can be seen
Between the end of infinite creations
Lies the mystical number thirteen

# 85. The very very tall man

The legend of Srinivasa Ramanujan
Shines like the Sun in the mathematical sky
All through the night and day
The mind of the genius had a life of own
The arms of creation had maths in them
Who ever could imagine the universe that way
The sorcerer of numbers and humble son of soil
The greatest pride of modern India
Alas died a poisonous death

# 86. The wise and solitary owl

The white owl flies silently like a smitten mountain breeze
Sparkling in the moonlight against the barren moony hills
Settling unseen in the high and dark deodar trees
It hoots and calls the creatures of the night times
At the darkest hour of the night when clouds come
The owl sings a song for the moon to return home
A lone wolf howls back into the winds of the autumn
And the owl blushes and shrugs to hear a fellow chum
The night sees the owl and the owl watches over the night
The old chiefs and the sad monks praise the wise owl white
Death cometh in the form of an owl sometimes they cite
And nothing is luckier if a traveler sees an owl in flight
They say the hills remember the wise owls that nested here
And souls of the dead owls come into hearts of the traveler
That they miss the lonely mountains and the moon all night
And howl in sad longings every time an owl calls hooot hoot

# 87. This sad day gets stuck in the night

This night is full of sadness I can feel
I doubt if I can sleep
A paradox it is to close my eyes and sleep
This night will be bitter
Showing the saddest movies of the past
I am too far from God's beautiful world
And my mind weighs heavy in sorrow
But regrets I have none
Except a few

# 88. To Mothers

In your hardest times
No one will care
Except your mother
Will always have kind words
And good old advice for you
Remember to call upon her
When your way gets darker than your thoughts

# 89. Unknown truth

Some questions burn at your soul
Asking questions about your soul
And you know nothing of the soul
Pity it is but let the truth be told
So that you may not let your soul
Be trapped in the world of humans
When death comes finally or unexpectedly
It is time that we have been waiting
For the holiest moment has come to meet God
Fire the elment of action and motion
Sends the soul to the kingdom of heaven
This is the ancient rule of creation
For the body to burn after death in cremation

# 90. Vedanta

In Vedanta we can take a part from whole
And the whole will still remain whole
In Vedanta something can be manifested from Nothing
As there is nothing such as nothing
In Vedanta you and I
Are not only not different
But exactly the same
In Vedanta we can never return to
From where we started
In Vedanta anything is never
Too far from something
In Vedanta the infinite reality lies
In the dimension of mind
In Vedanta Maya lies between the seen and unseen

# 91. Velocity of time

Sweet dreams mellow into sad reminiscences
Of a faithful lover into the wilderness
That beats in her heart always
As she leans slowly on her shoulders
To heal the poison in her neck
Her neat eyebrows wait
With ocean like dark eyes
For the past to replace her future
And seize control of the motion of time
Alas the time is not moving

# 92. Vultures of cultures

The cities in our countries grow bigger
And costlier every year
Eating the histories of times
And the people who toiled in it
Cutting through the bonds of old
And making new
That do not last long
The old fairs and the narrow streets
That last house in the row
The wild streams on the road
And cackles of laughter
The beautiful yellow flowers in the fields
And the warm sun above
Playing hide and seek with the clouds
They live now inside memories
Of forgotten times and cultures

# 93. Water to water

• 114 •

The human body comes from water and goes to water
Thus spake to his enrapt students the learned master
Between birth and death it flows in life through water
And in the ashes dissolved in water for the life after

# 94. When storm came in autumn

Golden lands shimmered
In the gift of autumn
And the air was transparent platinum
The children were fed
And the men and women
Rejoiced in their homes
Forgetful of all sorrows
The clouds huddled
And the birds flew noisily
The winds were slow
And the air felt silly
The circle of happiness
Surrounded all around me
Leaving me alone in the middle
Like a lonely lake far from the sea

# 95. When will the wild flowers bloom

The winds kissed merrily the wild flowers
And the flowers danced in wanton care
To the music of the long winding river
That slithered like a snake of sapphires
Under the innocent smiling face of the sky
The grassy slopes wore many hues of green
And the wild flowers of yellow white red blue purple
Twinkled like stars upon a greenish night
I must have been a flower in a past life
I wonder if I was lucky to have bloomed here
I remembered the flowers in my soul
Swinging in calming breezes of love
Pouring nectar into the air and spreading joy
Somethings have changed since then
The petals have become heavy
And the leaves no more hide the thorns
How jealous I feel of nature
My springs and summers do not come in time

# 96. Winter around the world

The sun is near and far
To somewhere
And winter and summer
Hide and seek
And play forever
Deep in the winter
People long for summer
But in the winter
Mother comes to earth
And takes care of her
Healing what summer scorched